Still Standing

Empowerment Journal
by
Ulaonda Parham, M.A.Ed

Believer • Fighter • Survivor.

Copyright © 2021 Ulaonda Parham
All Rights Reserved
No part of this publication may be reproduced, distributed or transmitted in any form or by any means, including photocopying recording, or other electronic or mechanical methods, without prior written permission from the author.

Still Standing, LLC
PO Box 1072
Clayton, NC 27520
www.ulaondaparham.com
ulaondaparham@gmail.com

ISBN: 978-0-5788241-3-0(paperback)
Library of Congress Control Number: 2021926067

Scripture quotations marked (NIV) are taken from the Holy Bible, New International Version®, NIV®. Copyright © 1973, 1978, 1984, 2011 by Biblica, Inc.® Used by permission of Zondervan. All rights reserved worldwide. www.zondervan.com The "NIV" and "New International Version" are trademarks registered in the United States Patent and Trademark Office by Biblica, Inc.®

Scripture quotations from The Authorized (King James) Version. Rights in the Authorized Version in the United Kingdom are vested in the Crown. Reproduced by permission of the Crown's patentee, Cambridge University Press

Cover Photo by Suave Visions

Special discounts are available on quantity purchases by corporations, associations, and others. For details, contact the author at ulaondaparham@gmail.com.

Message from the Author:

I Dedicate this Empowerment Journal To YOU.

You are Fearfully and Wonderfully Made! Never let people define who you are. You determine that. Whatever you do, do not ever compare yourself to others. Focus on becoming the best version of yourself. Be sure to spend some time with you because YOU matter too!

I wish you much success and love on your self-love journey.
-Ulaonda Parham, M.A.Ed.

*Chapter Me
Self-Love*

**STILL STANDING
EMPOWERMENT JOURNAL
BELONGS TO:**

_____

Monthly Self-Care Planner

JANUARY

♥ TODAY'S SELF-CARE GOAL:

♥ SELF-CARE TO-DO LIST

♥ SELF-CARE IMPORTANT NOTES:

Monthly Self-Care Planner

FEBRUARY

♥ TODAY'S SELF-CARE GOAL:

♥ SELF-CARE TO-DO LIST

♥ SELF-CARE IMPORTANT NOTES:

Monthly Self-Care Planner

MARCH

♥ TODAY'S SELF-CARE GOAL:

♥ SELF-CARE TO-DO LIST

♥ SELF-CARE IMPORTANT NOTES:

Monthly Self-Care Planner

APRIL

♥ TODAY'S SELF-CARE GOAL:

♥ SELF-CARE TO-DO LIST

♥ SELF-CARE IMPORTANT NOTES:

Monthly Self-Care Planner

MAY

♥ TODAY'S SELF-CARE GOAL:

♥ SELF-CARE TO-DO LIST

♥ SELF-CARE IMPORTANT NOTES:

Monthly Self-Care Planner

JUNE

♥ TODAY'S SELF-CARE GOAL:

♥ SELF-CARE TO-DO LIST

♥ SELF-CARE IMPORTANT NOTES:

Monthly Self-Care Planner
JULY

♥ TODAY'S SELF-CARE GOAL:

♥ SELF-CARE TO-DO LIST

♥ SELF-CARE IMPORTANT NOTES:

Monthly Self-Care Planner

AUGUST

♥ TODAY'S SELF-CARE GOAL:

♥ SELF-CARE TO-DO LIST

♥ SELF-CARE IMPORTANT NOTES:

Monthly Self-Care Planner

SEPTEMBER

♥ TODAY'S SELF-CARE GOAL:

♥ SELF-CARE TO-DO LIST

♥ SELF-CARE IMPORTANT NOTES:

Monthly Self-Care Planner

OCTOBER

♥ TODAY'S SELF-CARE GOAL:

♥ SELF-CARE TO-DO LIST

♥ SELF-CARE IMPORTANT NOTES:

Monthly Self-Care Planner

NOVEMBER

♥ TODAY'S SELF-CARE GOAL:

♥ SELF-CARE TO-DO LIST

♥ SELF-CARE IMPORTANT NOTES:

Monthly Self-Care Planner
DECEMBER

♥ TODAY'S SELF-CARE GOAL:

♥ SELF CARE TO-DO LIST

♥ SELF-CARE IMPORTANT NOTES:

SELF-LOVE AFFIRMATIONS

I AM NOT MY PAST

I AM FREE

I AM NOT MY TRAUMA

I AM THANKFUL

MEMORY LANE

"JESUS CHRIST IS THE SAME YESTERDAY AND TODAY AND FOREVER." HEBREW 13:8 NIV

1. As you walk down memory lane, ask yourself, do you want to go? Was your response lets go, I don't want to go, or was it a little of both? Write down your thoughts below...

_____

_____

_____

_____

2. After answering question number one, how do you feel?

_____

_____

_____

_____

_____

"JESUS CHRIST IS THE SAME YESTERDAY AND TODAY AND FOREVER." HEBREW 13:8 NIV

3. Write down ALL your emotions, define each one.

_____

_____

_____

_____

4. Did you understand the definitions of your feelings? Were you surprised?

_____

_____

_____

_____

"JESUS CHRIST IS THE SAME YESTERDAY AND TODAY AND FOREVER." HEBREW 13:8 NIV

5. Before answering the questions above, did you avoid going down your memory lane? Why or Why not?

_____

_____

_____

_____

6. Study the scripture reference Hebrew 13:8. What are the words saying to you when you read this?

_____

_____

_____

_____

"JESUS CHRIST IS THE SAME YESTERDAY AND TODAY AND FOREVER." HEBREW 13:8 NIV

7. How can you intentionally apply Hebrew 13:8 to your life? (take your time, this is your journey)

_____

_____

_____

_____

8. Was Hebrew 13:8 comforting, convicting, or neither? Explain...

_____

_____

_____

_____

Self-Love Affirmations

My mental wellness is a priority
I can eat healthier/exercise
I can rest more
I should laugh more

Mental Illness

> "I HAVE TOLD YOU THESE THINGS SO THAT IN ME YOU MAY HAVE PEACE. IN THIS WORLD YOU WILL HAVE TROUBLE. BUT TAKE HEART I HAVE OVERCOME THE WORLD."
> JOHN 16:33 NIV

1. Define mental illness.

_____

_____

_____

_____

2. What does mental illness mean to you?

_____

_____

_____

_____

_____

"I HAVE TOLD YOU THESE THINGS SO THAT IN ME YOU MAY HAVE PEACE. IN THIS WORLD YOU WILL HAVE TROUBLE. BUT TAKE HEART I HAVE OVERCOME THE WORLD."
JOHN 16:33 NIV

3. Do you feel comfortable with taking a mental health questionnaire?

(Disclaimer: this is not a medical accurate test;
it is only used for self-awareness)
If you answered Yes, the website is listed below:
https://screening.mhanational.org/screening-tools

If you answered No, that is okay! Take it whenever you are ready)

If you answered Yes, what do the results mean to you? Discuss...

_____
_____
_____
_____
_____
_____
_____
_____

"I HAVE TOLD YOU THESE THINGS SO THAT IN ME YOU MAY HAVE PEACE. IN THIS WORLD YOU WILL HAVE TROUBLE. BUT TAKE HEART I HAVE OVERCOME THE WORLD."
JOHN 16:33 NIV

4. According to your results, do you feel that you Need TO SEEK HELP? If your answer was yes, are you ok with seeing a therapist/counselor? Why or Why not?

_____

_____

_____

_____

5. How are counselors and therapists different/similar?

_____

_____

_____

_____

_____

"I HAVE TOLD YOU THESE THINGS SO THAT IN ME YOU MAY HAVE PEACE. IN THIS WORLD YOU WILL HAVE TROUBLE. BUT TAKE HEART I HAVE OVERCOME THE WORLD."
JOHN 16:33 NIV

6. How comfortable are you with speaking about mental illnesses? Circle: comfortable somewhat comfortable not comfortable. Why?

_____
_____
_____
_____

7. How comfortable are you with speaking about mental illnesses? Circle: comfortable somewhat comfortable not comfortable. Why?

_____
_____
_____
_____

"I HAVE TOLD YOU THESE THINGS SO THAT IN ME YOU MAY HAVE PEACE. IN THIS WORLD YOU WILL HAVE TROUBLE. BUT TAKE HEART I HAVE OVERCOME THE WORLD."
JOHN 16:33 NIV

8. Study the scripture reference John 16:33 What are the words saying to you when you read this?

_____
_____
_____
_____

9. How can you intentionally apply John 16:33 to your life?

_____
_____
_____
_____
_____

"I HAVE TOLD YOU THESE THINGS SO THAT IN ME YOU MAY HAVE PEACE. IN THIS WORLD YOU WILL HAVE TROUBLE. BUT TAKE HEART I HAVE OVERCOME THE WORLD."
JOHN 16:33 NIV

10. Was John 16:33 comforting, convicting, or neither? Explain...

_____

_____

_____

_____

_____

_____

_____

Self-Love Affirmations

I AM BRAVE

I CAN DO THIS

I AM A SURVIVOR

I AM AN OVERCOMER

Surviving

> "THIS IS WHAT THE LORD SAYS: THE PEOPLE
> WHO SURVIVE THE SWORD WILL FIND FAVOR IN
> THE WILDERNESS; I WILL COME TO GIVE REST TO ISRAEL."
> JEREMIAH 31:2 NIV

1. Define survival.

_____

_____

_____

_____

2. Describe your survival journey?

_____

_____

_____

_____

_____

> "THIS IS WHAT THE LORD SAYS: THE PEOPLE
> WHO SURVIVE THE SWORD WILL FIND FAVOR IN
> THE WILDERNESS; I WILL COME TO GIVE REST TO ISRAEL."
> JEREMIAH 31:2 NIV

3. Was it difficult for you to reflect on survival? Why or why not?

_____

_____

_____

_____

4. What does it mean to cope?

_____

_____

_____

_____

"THIS IS WHAT THE LORD SAYS: THE PEOPLE
WHO SURVIVE THE SWORD WILL FIND FAVOR IN
THE WILDERNESS; I WILL COME TO GIVE REST TO ISRAEL."
JEREMIAH 31:2 NIV

5. Define the four major coping mechanisms. Give examples of each.

Problem-focused-

_____
_____
_____
_____
_____

Emotion-focused-

_____
_____
_____
_____
_____

"THIS IS WHAT THE LORD SAYS: THE PEOPLE
WHO SURVIVE THE SWORD WILL FIND FAVOR IN
THE WILDERNESS; I WILL COME TO GIVE REST TO ISRAEL."
JEREMIAH 31:2 NIV

Meaning-focused-

_____
_____
_____
_____
_____

Social coping- (support seeking)

_____
_____
_____
_____
_____

"THIS IS WHAT THE LORD SAYS: THE PEOPLE
WHO SURVIVE THE SWORD WILL FIND FAVOR IN
THE WILDERNESS; I WILL COME TO GIVE REST TO ISRAEL."
JEREMIAH 31:2 NIV

6. List some of your coping mechanisms. (Be honest this is your unique journey, and you should be proud of your resilience)

_____

_____

_____

_____

7. Did you experience childhood trauma? if so, have you triumphed over your trauma: or have you intentionally avoided your trauma experiences? (it is your journey...answer whenever you are ready to have this conversation with yourself.)

_____

_____

_____

_____

"THIS IS WHAT THE LORD SAYS: THE PEOPLE WHO SURVIVE THE SWORD WILL FIND FAVOR IN THE WILDERNESS; I WILL COME TO GIVE REST TO ISRAEL."
JEREMIAH 31:2 NIV

8. Study the scripture reference Jeremiah 31:2. What are the words saying to you when you read this?

_____

_____

_____

_____

9. How can you intentionally apply Jeremiah 31:2 to your life?

_____

_____

_____

_____

"THIS IS WHAT THE LORD SAYS: THE PEOPLE
WHO SURVIVE THE SWORD WILL FIND FAVOR IN
THE WILDERNESS; I WILL COME TO GIVE REST TO ISRAEL."
JEREMIAH 31:2 NIV

10. Was Jeremiah 31:2 comforting, convicting, or neither? Explain...

_____

_____

_____

_____

_____

_____

_____

Self-Love Affirmations
I forgive me
My body/mind can be healed
I am powerful
I will shift my mindset

Healing/healed

"BEHOLD, I WILL BRING IT HEALTH AND CURE, AND I WILL CURE THEM, AND WILL REVEAL UNTO THEM THE ABUNDANCE OF PEACE AND TRUTH."
JEREMIAH 33:6 KJV

1. Have you or anyone close to you been physically or mentally ill? Describe your experiences.

_____
_____
_____
_____

2. Do you believe faith alone can heal you? Why or why not?

_____
_____
_____
_____

"BEHOLD, I WILL BRING IT HEALTH AND CURE, AND I WILL CURE THEM, AND WILL REVEAL UNTO THEM THE ABUNDANCE OF PEACE AND TRUTH."
JEREMIAH 33:6 KJV

3. Is it possible to be healed by a combination of God, medicine, and a healthy diet? Explain...

_____

_____

_____

_____

4. Study the scripture reference Jeremiah 33:6. What are the words saying to you when you read this?

_____

_____

_____

_____

> "BEHOLD, I WILL BRING IT HEALTH AND CURE, AND I WILL CURE THEM, AND WILL REVEAL UNTO THEM THE ABUNDANCE OF PEACE AND TRUTH."
> JEREMIAH 33:6 KJV

5. How can you intentionally apply Jeremiah 33:6 to your life?

_____

_____

_____

_____

6. Was Jeremiah 33:6 comforting, convicting, or neither? Explain...

_____

_____

_____

_____

SELF-LOVE AFFIRMATIONS

I AM SUCCESSFUL

FAITH OVER FEARS

TRUST THE PROCESS

I AM WORTH IT

NEW ADVENTURE

"HAVE NOT I COMMANDED THEE? BE STRONG
AND OF GOOD COURAGE. BE NOT AFRAID,
NEITHER BE THOU DISMAYED: FOR THE LORD
THY GOD IS WITH THEE WHITHERSOEVER THOU GOEST."
JOSHUA 1:9 KJV

1. Are you in your comfort zone? Are you happy there? Explain...

_____

_____

_____

_____

2. Make a list of your goals...

_____

_____

_____

_____

"HAVE NOT I COMMANDED THEE? BE STRONG
AND OF GOOD COURAGE. BE NOT AFRAID,
NEITHER BE THOU DISMAYED: FOR THE LORD
THY GOD IS WITH THEE WHITHERSOEVER THOU GOEST."
JOSHUA 1:9 KJV

3. Have you achieved any of your goals? Did you achieve any in your comfort zone? How? If not are you okay with this? Explain...

_____
_____
_____
_____

4. Make a list of your fears. (be honest with you)

_____
_____
_____
_____

"HAVE NOT I COMMANDED THEE? BE STRONG
AND OF GOOD COURAGE. BE NOT AFRAID,
NEITHER BE THOU DISMAYED: FOR THE LORD
THY GOD IS WITH THEE WHITHERSOEVER THOU GOEST."
JOSHUA 1:9 KJV

5. Your list of fears represents what "stepping out" of your comfort zone looks like. Do you agree or disagree? Explain...

_____

_____

_____

_____

6. Study the scripture reference Joshua 1:9. What are the words saying to you when you read this?

_____

_____

_____

_____

"HAVE NOT I COMMANDED THEE? BE STRONG
AND OF GOOD COURAGE. BE NOT AFRAID,
NEITHER BE THOU DISMAYED: FOR THE LORD
THY GOD IS WITH THEE WHITHERSOEVER THOU GOEST."
JOSHUA 1:9 KJV

7. How can you intentionally apply Joshua 1:9 to your life?

_____

_____

_____

_____

8. Was Joshua 1:9 comforting, convicting, or neither? Explain...

_____

_____

_____

_____

_____

Self-Love Affirmations

MY FEELINGS ARE VALID
I GIVE MYSELF TIME TO GRIEVE
MY PAIN IS TEMPORARY
I HAVE MORE REASONS TO SMILE

Pain

"AND GOD SHALL WIPE AWAY ALL TEARS FROM THEIR EYES; AND THERE SHALL BE NO MORE DEATH, NEITHER SORROW, NOR CRYING, NEITHER SHALL THERE BE ANY MORE PAIN: FOR THE FORMER THINGS ARE PASSED AWAY." REVELATION 21:4 KJV

1. Have you experienced pain or are you experiencing pain? Write down your painful experiences.

_____

_____

_____

_____

2. Was it difficult? Did you skip number one?

(If so, it is okay. Give yourself time. Identifying pain is an important part of your healing journey.)

If you wrote down your painful moments, make a list of your feelings. Do you understand your feelings? Share your thoughts

_____

_____

_____

_____

"AND GOD SHALL WIPE AWAY ALL TEARS FROM THEIR EYES; AND THERE SHALL BE NO MORE DEATH, NEITHER SORROW, NOR CRYING, NEITHER SHALL THERE BE ANY MORE PAIN: FOR THE FORMER THINGS ARE PASSED AWAY." REVELATION 21:4 KJV

3. Are you okay? ____ Pain is a tough topic to talk about... Give yourself time. Take a break... Remember acknowledging pain or any feelings is progress. This is your unique journey. Do what you need to do to cope.

If your answer was yes, share your experiences on reaching such a difficult breakthrough.

_____

_____

_____

_____

4. List some ways that you cope when dealing with pain? Be true to yourself!

_____

_____

_____

_____

AND GOD SHALL WIPE AWAY ALL TEARS FROM THEIR EYES; AND THERE SHALL BE NO MORE DEATH, NEITHER SORROW, NOR CRYING, NEITHER SHALL THERE BE ANY MORE PAIN: FOR THE FORMER THINGS ARE PASSED AWAY." REVELATION 21:4 KJV

5. Have you ever experienced grief from the death of a loved one? Did you get grief support?

_____

_____

_____

_____

6. Did you turn to alcohol, drugs, sex, food, work, exercise, prayer, journaling, meditation, counseling, friends/family, or etc? Circle all that apply. How do you feel about your choice(s) of coping mechanisms? Did they help? Explain...

_____

_____

_____

_____

AND GOD SHALL WIPE AWAY ALL TEARS FROM THEIR EYES; AND THERE SHALL BE NO MORE DEATH, NEITHER SORROW, NOR CRYING, NEITHER SHALL THERE BE ANY MORE PAIN: FOR THE FORMER THINGS ARE PASSED AWAY." REVELATION 21:4 KJV

7. Did you turn to God?

Did you get closer to God?

Do you believe in God?

Did you find God?

Are you mad at God?

Did you turn away from God?

Discuss your answers.

_____

_____

_____

_____

8. Study the scripture reference Revelation 21:4. What are the words saying to you when you read this?

_____

_____

_____

_____

AND GOD SHALL WIPE AWAY ALL TEARS FROM THEIR EYES; AND THERE SHALL BE NO MORE DEATH, NEITHER SORROW, NOR CRYING, NEITHER SHALL THERE BE ANY MORE PAIN: FOR THE FORMER THINGS ARE PASSED AWAY." REVELATION 21:4 KJV

9. How can you intentionally apply Revelation 21:4 to your life?

_____

_____

_____

_____

10. Was Revelation 21:4 comforting, convicting, or neither? Explain...

_____

_____

_____

_____

Self-Love Affirmations
I LOVE ME
I AM IMPERFECT....AND THAT'S OK
I AM ENOUGH
I CHOOSE LOVE OVER HATE

New Love

"ABOVE ALL,
LOVE EACH OTHER DEEPLY, BECAUSE LOVE COVERS
OVER A MULTITUDE OF SINS." 1 PETER 4:8 NIV

1. Define love.

_____
_____
_____
_____

2. Make a list of some things you love. **Do them!

_____
_____
_____
_____
_____

"ABOVE ALL, LOVE EACH OTHER DEEPLY, BECAUSE LOVE COVERS OVER A MULTITUDE OF SINS." 1 PETER 4:8 NIV

3. What are some of the "surprise" experiences you had in your life? What are some things you told yourself that you would never do, but you did it?

_____

_____

_____

_____

4. What are some of the "unwanted" surprises that happened to you in your life? Have you grown from them?

_____

_____

_____

_____

> "ABOVE ALL,
> LOVE EACH OTHER DEEPLY, BECAUSE LOVE COVERS
> OVER A MULTITUDE OF SINS." 1 PETER 4:8 NIV

5. If you are a single parent or was raised by a single parent; do you feel broken or that you failed? Describe your thoughts. (remember all your feelings are valid and important) Express yourself...

_____
_____
_____
_____

6. Are you influenced by social media/society's expectations for your life? Are you okay with your answer? Explain...

_____
_____
_____
_____
_____

"ABOVE ALL, LOVE EACH OTHER DEEPLY, BECAUSE LOVE COVERS OVER A MULTITUDE OF SINS." 1 PETER 4:8 NIV

7. Have you ever felt as if you were living in someone else's shadow? As if you did not know who you were because you were living to family and friends' expectations. How does this make you feel? List some ways that you can switch the focus to yourself instead?

_____

_____

_____

_____

8. What are some ways that you can focus on individualizing your beliefs? How can you embrace your ideas and implement them in your life?

_____

_____

_____

_____

"ABOVE ALL, LOVE EACH OTHER DEEPLY, BECAUSE LOVE COVERS OVER A MULTITUDE OF SINS." 1 PETER 4:8 NIV

9. Study the scripture reference 1 Peter 4:8. What are the words saying to you when you read this?

_____

_____

_____

_____

10. How can you intentionally apply 1 Peter 4:8 to your life?

_____

_____

_____

_____

_____

Self-Love Affirmations
I AM A FIGHTER
I AM A CHILD OF A KING
I AM CONTENT
I WILL NEVER GIVE UP

Strength

"I CAN DO ALL THINGS THROUGH CHRIST WHICH STRENGTHENETH ME." PHILIPPIANS 4:13 KJV

1. Define strength.

_____

_____

_____

_____

2. Do you consider yourself strong? Why or why not?

_____

_____

_____

_____

"I CAN DO ALL THINGS THROUGH CHRIST WHICH STRENGTHENETH ME." PHILIPPIANS 4:13 KJV

3. Is there a connection between your pain and strength? Explain...

_____
_____
_____
_____

4. Do you think strength is a good characteristic to have? Explain...

_____
_____
_____
_____

"I CAN DO ALL THINGS THROUGH CHRIST WHICH STRENGTHENETH ME." PHILIPPIANS 4:13 KJV

5. Write down some ways you consider yourself strong.

_____

_____

_____

_____

6. If your list was short, do you think this makes you weak? Why or why not?

_____

_____

_____

_____

"I CAN DO ALL THINGS THROUGH CHRIST WHICH STRENGTHENETH ME." PHILIPPIANS 4:13 KJV

7. Make a list of your strengths/weaknesses.

_____

_____

_____

_____

8. Rate yourself based on your thoughts on where you stand regarding strength in each of these areas. Discuss your answers...

Mentally 1 2 3 4 5 6 7 8 9 10
Spiritually 1 2 3 4 5 6 7 8 9 10
Physically 1 2 3 4 5 6 7 8 9 10
Financially 1 2 3 4 5 6 7 8 9 10

_____

_____

_____

_____

"I CAN DO ALL THINGS THROUGH CHRIST WHICH STRENGTHENETH ME." PHILIPPIANS 4:13 KJV

9. Write down strategies you will work on to improve your ratings

_____

_____

_____

_____

10. Study the scripture reference Philippians 4:13. What are the words saying to you when you read this?

_____

_____

_____

_____

_____

"I CAN DO ALL THINGS THROUGH CHRIST WHICH STRENGTHENETH ME." PHILIPPIANS 4:13 KJV

11. How can you intentionally apply Philippians 4:13 to your life?

_____
_____
_____
_____

12. Was Philippians 4:13 comforting, convicting, or neither? Explain...

_____
_____
_____
_____
_____

Self-Love Affirmations

I BELIEVE IN ME
I AM CAPABLE
I LIVE BY FAITH...NOT BY SIGHT
I TRUST GOD

Faith

"FOR WE WALK BY FAITH, NOT BY SIGHT."
2 CORINTHIANS 5:7 KJV

1. Define faith.

_____

_____

_____

_____

2. What is your definition of faith?

_____

_____

_____

_____

"FOR WE WALK BY FAITH, NOT BY SIGHT."
2 CORINTHIANS 5:7 KJV

3. Do you think you can have faith and not be spiritual or believe in God? Explain...

_____

_____

_____

_____

4. Do you think it is good to have faith in people? Why or Why not?

_____

_____

_____

_____

"FOR WE WALK BY FAITH, NOT BY SIGHT."
2 CORINTHIANS 5:7 KJV

5. How can you increase your faith?

_____
_____
_____
_____

6. Is there a connection between patience and faith? Explain...

_____
_____
_____
_____

"FOR WE WALK BY FAITH, NOT BY SIGHT."
2 CORINTHIANS 5:7 KJV

7. List some ways that you can improve your patience.

_____
_____
_____
_____

8. What does the term "testing your faith" mean to you?

_____
_____
_____
_____

"FOR WE WALK BY FAITH, NOT BY SIGHT."
2 CORINTHIANS 5:7 KJV

9. Study the scripture reference 2 Corinthians 5:7. What are the words saying to you when you read this?

_____
_____
_____
_____

10. How can you intentionally apply 2 Corinthians 5:7 to life?

_____
_____
_____
_____
_____

"FOR WE WALK BY FAITH, NOT BY SIGHT."
2 CORINTHIANS 5:7 KJV

11. Was 2 Corinthians 5:7 comforting, convicting, or neither? Explain...

_____
_____
_____
_____
_____
_____
_____
_____

Self-Love Affirmations

I AM MY BIGGEST CHEERLEADER
I DESERVE TO REACH MY GOALS
I WANT THE BEST FOR ME
I GOT THIS

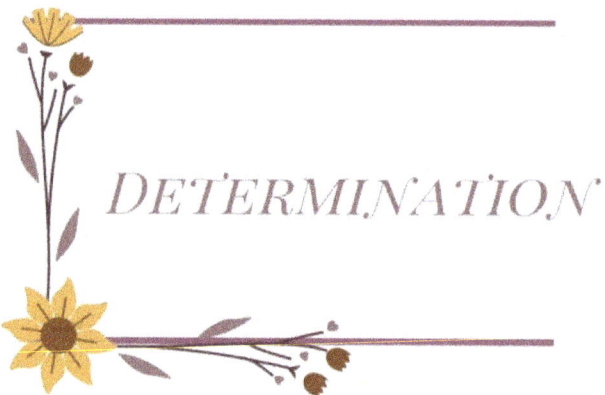

Determination

"FOR I KNOW THE THOUGHTS THAT I THINK TOWARDS YOU, SAITH THE LORD, THOUGHTS OF PEACE, AND NOT OF EVIL, TO GIVE YOU AN EXPECTED END."
JEREMIAH 29:11 KJV

1. Define determination.

_____

_____

_____

_____

2. What does it mean to have self-determination? Do you consider yourself to be a determined person? Are you okay with your answer? Explain...

_____

_____

_____

_____

_____

"FOR I KNOW THE THOUGHTS THAT I THINK TOWARDS YOU, SAITH THE LORD, THOUGHTS OF PEACE, AND NOT OF EVIL, TO GIVE YOU AN EXPECTED END."
JEREMIAH 29:11 KJV

3. What are goals and why are they important?

_____

_____

_____

_____

4. Make a list of all the goals you have had in your lifetime. Place a check on all of the ones you have achieved, underline the ones you are working on, and circle the ones that are no longer your goals.

_____

_____

_____

_____

_____

"FOR I KNOW THE THOUGHTS THAT I THINK TOWARDS YOU, SAITH THE LORD, THOUGHTS OF PEACE, AND NOT OF EVIL, TO GIVE YOU AN EXPECTED END."
JEREMIAH 29:11 KJV

5. What are some of the factors that have kept you from reaching your goals?

_____

_____

_____

_____

6. Do you lack confidence, knowledge, or motivation to reach your goals? If your answer was yes, do you believe there is a solution to your answer?

_____

_____

_____

_____

_____

"FOR I KNOW THE THOUGHTS THAT I THINK TOWARDS YOU, SAITH THE LORD, THOUGHTS OF PEACE, AND NOT OF EVIL, TO GIVE YOU AN EXPECTED END."
JEREMIAH 29:11 KJV

7. Do you feel that you are worthy of achieving your goals? Explain..

_____
_____
_____
_____

8. Define motivation? Do you see a connection with determination? Explain...

_____
_____
_____
_____

"FOR I KNOW THE THOUGHTS THAT I THINK TOWARDS YOU, SAITH THE LORD, THOUGHTS OF PEACE, AND NOT OF EVIL, TO GIVE YOU AN EXPECTED END."
JEREMIAH 29:11 KJV

9. Study the scripture reference Jeremiah 29:11. What are the words saying to you when you read this?

_____

_____

_____

_____

10. How can you intentionally apply Jeremiah 29:11 to life?

_____

_____

_____

_____

> FOR I KNOW THE THOUGHTS THAT I THINK TOWARDS YOU, SAITH THE LORD, THOUGHTS OF PEACE, AND NOT OF EVIL, TO GIVE YOU AN EXPECTED END."
> JEREMIAH 29:11 KJV

11. Was Jeremiah 29:11 comforting, convicting, or neither? Explain...

_____

_____

_____

_____

_____

_____

_____

_____

SELF-LOVE AFFIRMATIONS

I HOLD MYSELF ACCOUNTABLE

I WILL PREPARE FOR MY/FAMILY FUTURE

I WILL ADJUST TO CHANGE

PREPARATION

"THE LORD IS MY SHEPHERD; I SHALL NOT WANT.
HE MAKETH ME TO LIE DOWN IN GREEN PASTURES:
HE LEADETH ME BESIDE THE STILL WATERS.
HE RESTORETH MY SOUL: HE LEADETH ME IN THE PATHS
OF RIGHTEOUSNESS FOR HIS NAME SAKE.
YEA, THOUGH I WALK THROUGH THE VALLEY OF THE
SHADOW OF DEATH, I WILL FEAR NO EVIL: FOR THOU ART
WITH ME; THY ROD AND THY STAFF THEY COMFORT ME.
THOU PREPAREST A TABLE BEFORE ME IN THE
PRESENCE OF MINE ENEMIES: THOU ANOINTEST MY HEAD
WITH OIL; MY CUP RUNNETH OVER.
SURELY GOODNESS AND MERCY
SHALL FOLLOW ME ALL THE DAYS OF MY LIFE: AND I WILL
DWELL IN THE HOUSE OF THE LORD FOREVER." PSALM 23 1-
6 KJV

1. Define preparation.

_____

_____

_____

_____

_____

"THE LORD IS MY SHEPHERD; I SHALL NOT WANT.
HE MAKETH ME TO LIE DOWN IN GREEN PASTURES:
HE LEADETH ME BESIDE THE STILL WATERS.
HE RESTORETH MY SOUL: HE LEADETH ME IN THE PATHS
OF RIGHTEOUSNESS FOR HIS NAME SAKE.
YEA, THOUGH I WALK THROUGH THE VALLEY OF THE
SHADOW OF DEATH, I WILL FEAR NO EVIL: FOR THOU ART
WITH ME; THY ROD AND THY STAFF THEY COMFORT ME.
THOU PREPAREST A TABLE BEFORE ME IN THE
PRESENCE OF MINE ENEMIES: THOU ANOINTEST MY HEAD
WITH OIL; MY CUP RUNNETH OVER.
SURELY GOODNESS AND MERCY
SHALL FOLLOW ME ALL THE DAYS OF MY LIFE: AND I WILL
DWELL IN THE HOUSE OF THE LORD FOREVER." PSALM 23 1-
6 KJV

2. What does it mean "to prepare"? How important is it to you to prepare for the unexpected? (ex. Repairs, death, sickness) Explain...

_____

_____

_____

_____

_____

"THE LORD IS MY SHEPHERD; I SHALL NOT WANT.
HE MAKETH ME TO LIE DOWN IN GREEN PASTURES:
HE LEADETH ME BESIDE THE STILL WATERS.
HE RESTORETH MY SOUL: HE LEADETH ME IN THE PATHS OF RIGHTEOUSNESS FOR HIS NAME SAKE.
YEA, THOUGH I WALK THROUGH THE VALLEY OF THE SHADOW OF DEATH, I WILL FEAR NO EVIL: FOR THOU ART WITH ME; THY ROD AND THY STAFF THEY COMFORT ME.
THOU PREPAREST A TABLE BEFORE ME IN THE PRESENCE OF MINE ENEMIES: THOU ANOINTEST MY HEAD WITH OIL; MY CUP RUNNETH OVER.
SURELY GOODNESS AND MERCY
SHALL FOLLOW ME ALL THE DAYS OF MY LIFE: AND I WILL DWELL IN THE HOUSE OF THE LORD FOREVER.." PSALM 23 1-6 KJV

3. What are some ways you prepare for you and your family?

_____

_____

_____

_____

"THE LORD IS MY SHEPHERD; I SHALL NOT WANT.
HE MAKETH ME TO LIE DOWN IN GREEN PASTURES:
HE LEADETH ME BESIDE THE STILL WATERS.
HE RESTORETH MY SOUL; HE LEADETH ME IN THE PATHS
OF RIGHTEOUSNESS FOR HIS NAME SAKE.
YEA, THOUGH I WALK THROUGH THE VALLEY OF THE
SHADOW OF DEATH, I WILL FEAR NO EVIL: FOR THOU ART
WITH ME; THY ROD AND THY STAFF THEY COMFORT ME.
THOU PREPAREST A TABLE BEFORE ME IN THE
PRESENCE OF MINE ENEMIES: THOU ANOINTEST MY HEAD
WITH OIL; MY CUP RUNNETH OVER.
SURELY GOODNESS AND MERCY
SHALL FOLLOW ME ALL THE DAYS OF MY LIFE: AND I WILL
DWELL IN THE HOUSE OF THE LORD FOREVER." PSALM 23 1-
6 KJV

4. Are all preparations good? Why or why not?

_____

_____

_____

_____

_____

"THE LORD IS MY SHEPHERD; I SHALL NOT WANT.
HE MAKETH ME TO LIE DOWN IN GREEN PASTURES:
HE LEADETH ME BESIDE THE STILL WATERS.
HE RESTORETH MY SOUL: HE LEADETH ME IN THE PATHS OF RIGHTEOUSNESS FOR HIS NAME SAKE.
YEA, THOUGH I WALK THROUGH THE VALLEY OF THE SHADOW OF DEATH, I WILL FEAR NO EVIL: FOR THOU ART WITH ME; THY ROD AND THY STAFF THEY COMFORT ME.
THOU PREPAREST A TABLE BEFORE ME IN THE PRESENCE OF MINE ENEMIES: THOU ANOINTEST MY HEAD WITH OIL; MY CUP RUNNETH OVER.
SURELY GOODNESS AND MERCY
SHALL FOLLOW ME ALL THE DAYS OF MY LIFE: AND I WILL DWELL IN THE HOUSE OF THE LORD FOREVER.." PSALM 23 1-6 KJV

5. Make a list of preparations you would like to prepare for...

"THE LORD IS MY SHEPHERD; I SHALL NOT WANT.
HE MAKETH ME TO LIE DOWN IN GREEN PASTURES:
HE LEADETH ME BESIDE THE STILL WATERS.
HE RESTORETH MY SOUL: HE LEADETH ME IN THE PATHS
OF RIGHTEOUSNESS FOR HIS NAME SAKE.
YEA, THOUGH I WALK THROUGH THE VALLEY OF THE
SHADOW OF DEATH, I WILL FEAR NO EVIL: FOR THOU ART
WITH ME; THY ROD AND THY STAFF THEY COMFORT ME.
THOU PREPAREST A TABLE BEFORE ME IN THE
PRESENCE OF MINE ENEMIES: THOU ANOINTEST MY HEAD
WITH OIL; MY CUP RUNNETH OVER.
SURELY GOODNESS AND MERCY
SHALL FOLLOW ME ALL THE DAYS OF MY LIFE: AND I WILL
DWELL IN THE HOUSE OF THE LORD FOREVER.." PSALM 23 1-
6 KJV

6. Do you have life insurance? Why or why not?

_____

_____

_____

_____

"THE LORD IS MY SHEPHERD; I SHALL NOT WANT.
HE MAKETH ME TO LIE DOWN IN GREEN PASTURES:
HE LEADETH ME BESIDE THE STILL WATERS.
HE RESTORETH MY SOUL: HE LEADETH ME IN THE PATHS OF RIGHTEOUSNESS FOR HIS NAME SAKE.
YEA, THOUGH I WALK THROUGH THE VALLEY OF THE SHADOW OF DEATH, I WILL FEAR NO EVIL: FOR THOU ART WITH ME; THY ROD AND THY STAFF THEY COMFORT ME.
THOU PREPAREST A TABLE BEFORE ME IN THE PRESENCE OF MINE ENEMIES: THOU ANOINTEST MY HEAD WITH OIL; MY CUP RUNNETH OVER.
SURELY GOODNESS AND MERCY
SHALL FOLLOW ME ALL THE DAYS OF MY LIFE: AND I WILL DWELL IN THE HOUSE OF THE LORD FOREVER." PSALM 23 1-6 KJV

7. How can you be intentional about preparing for your death? Write out a plan of action.

_____

_____

_____

_____

"THE LORD IS MY SHEPHERD; I SHALL NOT WANT.
HE MAKETH ME TO LIE DOWN IN GREEN PASTURES:
HE LEADETH ME BESIDE THE STILL WATERS.
HE RESTORETH MY SOUL: HE LEADETH ME IN THE PATHS
OF RIGHTEOUSNESS FOR HIS NAME SAKE.
YEA, THOUGH I WALK THROUGH THE VALLEY OF THE
SHADOW OF DEATH, I WILL FEAR NO EVIL: FOR THOU ART
WITH ME; THY ROD AND THY STAFF THEY COMFORT ME.
THOU PREPAREST A TABLE BEFORE ME IN THE
PRESENCE OF MINE ENEMIES: THOU ANOINTEST MY HEAD
WITH OIL; MY CUP RUNNETH OVER.
SURELY GOODNESS AND MERCY
SHALL FOLLOW ME ALL THE DAYS OF MY LIFE: AND I WILL
DWELL IN THE HOUSE OF THE LORD FOREVER." PSALM 23 1-
6 KJV

8. Study the scripture reference Psalm 23 1-6. What are the words saying to you when you read this?

_____

_____

_____

_____

_____

"THE LORD IS MY SHEPHERD; I SHALL NOT WANT.
HE MAKETH ME TO LIE DOWN IN GREEN PASTURES:
HE LEADETH ME BESIDE THE STILL WATERS.
HE RESTORETH MY SOUL: HE LEADETH ME IN THE PATHS OF RIGHTEOUSNESS FOR HIS NAME SAKE.
YEA, THOUGH I WALK THROUGH THE VALLEY OF THE SHADOW OF DEATH, I WILL FEAR NO EVIL: FOR THOU ART WITH ME; THY ROD AND THY STAFF THEY COMFORT ME.
THOU PREPAREST A TABLE BEFORE ME IN THE PRESENCE OF MINE ENEMIES: THOU ANOINTEST MY HEAD WITH OIL; MY CUP RUNNETH OVER.
SURELY GOODNESS AND MERCY
SHALL FOLLOW ME ALL THE DAYS OF MY LIFE: AND I WILL DWELL IN THE HOUSE OF THE LORD FOREVER." PSALM 23 1-6 KJV

9. How can you intentionally apply Psalm 23 1-6 to life?

_____

_____

_____

_____

"THE LORD IS MY SHEPHERD; I SHALL NOT WANT.
HE MAKETH ME TO LIE DOWN IN GREEN PASTURES:
HE LEADETH ME BESIDE THE STILL WATERS.
HE RESTORETH MY SOUL: HE LEADETH ME IN THE PATHS
OF RIGHTEOUSNESS FOR HIS NAME SAKE.
YEA, THOUGH I WALK THROUGH THE VALLEY OF THE
SHADOW OF DEATH, I WILL FEAR NO EVIL: FOR THOU ART
WITH ME; THY ROD AND THY STAFF THEY COMFORT ME.
THOU PREPAREST A TABLE BEFORE ME IN THE
PRESENCE OF MINE ENEMIES: THOU ANOINTEST MY HEAD
WITH OIL; MY CUP RUNNETH OVER.
SURELY GOODNESS AND MERCY
SHALL FOLLOW ME ALL THE DAYS OF MY LIFE: AND I WILL
DWELL IN THE HOUSE OF THE LORD FOREVER." PSALM 23 1-
6 KJV

10. Was Psalm 23 1-6 comforting, convicting, or neither? Explain...

_____

_____

_____

_____

_____

Self-Love Affirmations

I AM CALM/RELAXED

EXERCISE IS GOOD FOR MY MIND

I WILL LET GO OF THE THINGS I CANNOT CONTROL

PEACE

"*"PEACE I LEAVE WITH YOU, MY PEACE I GIVE UNTO YOU: NOT AS THE WORLD GIVETH, GIVE I UNTO YOU. LET NOT YOUR HEART BE TROUBLED, NEITHER LET IT BE AFRAID."
JOHN 14:27 KJV*

1. Define peace.

_____

_____

_____

_____

2. Are you currently at peace? Describe this feeling...

_____

_____

_____

_____

""PEACE I LEAVE WITH YOU, MY PEACE I GIVE UNTO YOU:
NOT AS THE WORLD GIVETH, GIVE I UNTO YOU. LET NOT
YOUR HEART BE TROUBLED, NEITHER LET IT BE AFRAID."
JOHN 14:27 KJV

3. What are some ways you obtain peace?

_____
_____
_____
_____

4. How do you maintain your peaceful state of mind?

_____
_____
_____
_____

""PEACE I LEAVE WITH YOU, MY PEACE I GIVE UNTO YOU: NOT AS THE WORLD GIVETH, GIVE I UNTO YOU. LET NOT YOUR HEART BE TROUBLED, NEITHER LET IT BE AFRAID." JOHN 14:27 KJV

5. Make a list of things that brought/bring you peace?

_____
_____
_____
_____

6. What are some things that interfere with your peace? (try to avoid if possible)

_____
_____
_____
_____

> "'PEACE I LEAVE WITH YOU, MY PEACE I GIVE UNTO YOU: NOT AS THE WORLD GIVETH, GIVE I UNTO YOU. LET NOT YOUR HEART BE TROUBLED, NEITHER LET IT BE AFRAID."
> JOHN 14:27 KJV

7. What does "guard your heart" mean? What are some ways that you can be more intentional about guarding your heart?

_____

_____

_____

_____

8. Make a list of the things that you CAN control in your life.

_____

_____

_____

_____

""PEACE I LEAVE WITH YOU, MY PEACE I GIVE UNTO YOU: NOT AS THE WORLD GIVETH, GIVE I UNTO YOU. LET NOT YOUR HEART BE TROUBLED, NEITHER LET IT BE AFRAID."
JOHN 14:27 KJV

9. Make a list of the things you CANNOT control in your life. Note: Be intentional with not allowing those things that you cannot control to interfere with disturbing your peace. (I personally pray in advance for God to help prepare me mentally, physically, emotionally, and financially for these uncontrollable things.)

_____

_____

_____

_____

_____

10. Study the scripture reference John 14:27. What are the words saying to you when you read this?

_____

_____

_____

_____

_____

> "'PEACE I LEAVE WITH YOU, MY PEACE I GIVE UNTO YOU: NOT AS THE WORLD GIVETH, GIVE I UNTO YOU. LET NOT YOUR HEART BE TROUBLED, NEITHER LET IT BE AFRAID."
> JOHN 14:27 KJV

11. How can you intentionally apply Psalm 23 1-6 to life?

_____

_____

_____

_____

12. Was Psalm 23 1-6 comforting, convicting, or neither? Explain...

_____

_____

_____

_____

_____

Journal Prompts

1. If I could talk to my younger self, what would I say?
2. Make a list of at least 20 things that make me smile...
3. Who am I? Describe yourself using at least 15 words...
4. Make a list of at least 20 things that make me angry...
5. I'm so sick of...
6. What activities make me calm...
7. When I'm in pain (emotional, physical, mental) what is the nicest thing I can do for myself...
8. I am thankful for...
9. What is a habit that I love the most?
10. What keeps me awake at night?
11. Write a thank you letter to someone...
12. My dream career looks like...
13. How do I deal with anger?
14. Am I comfortable with being alone?
15. What will make the world a better place?

Journal Prompts

16. I am most confident when...
17. What is unique about me?
18. I need more...
19. What parts of my life need improving?
20. What is bothering me right now?
21. I can love myself more by...
22. If I was given $100,000 I would...
23. What self-love habit do I want to start?
24. How does being abandoned affect me?
25. What brings me joy?
26. How do I handle conflict?
27. If I could open up a business, what will it be?
28. Write me a thank you letter...
29. How do I recharge?
30. What am I interested in learning more about?
31. Write about my favorite animal...
32. What helps me slow down?
33. How can I be more present for me/family?
34. How do I put myself first without feeling guilty?
35. How do I advocate for myself?

Journal Prompts

36. Make a list of 10 things that make me cry...
37. My most important boundaries are...
38. How do I protect my boundaries?
39. How do I stay focused and steer clear of distractions?
40. Write about a teacher or coach who has inspired me...
41. What is the best part of quarantine?
42. What is the worst part of quarantine?
43. What do I need to do more of?
44. Do I have a childhood trauma that I never healed from?
45. Name one thing that I look forward to each day?
46. What is a habit that I dislike the most?
47. What habit do I need to incorporate into my life?
48. What does my anxiety feel like?
49. I will never forget this moment in my life...
50. How do I embrace my authentic self, even when it looks different?

I LOVE ME
Tell YOU Something Good...

I LOVE ME
Tell YOU Something Good...

_____

_____

_____

_____

_____

_____

_____

_____

_____

I LOVE ME
Tell YOU Something Good...

_____

_____

_____

_____

_____

_____

_____

_____

I LOVE ME
Tell YOU Something Good...

_____

_____

_____

_____

_____

_____

_____

_____

_____

I LOVE ME
Tell YOU Something Good...

I LOVE ME
Tell YOU Something Good...

_____

_____

_____

_____

_____

_____

_____

_____

_____

I LOVE ME
Tell YOU Something Good...

_____

_____

_____

_____

_____

_____

_____

_____

I LOVE ME
Tell YOU Something Good...

I LOVE ME
Tell YOU Something Good…

_____
_____
_____
_____
_____
_____
_____
_____

I LOVE ME
Tell YOU Something Good...

_____

_____

_____

_____

_____

_____

_____

_____

I LOVE ME
Tell YOU Something Good...

I LOVE ME
Tell YOU Something Good...

_____

_____

_____

_____

_____

_____

_____

_____

_____

I LOVE ME
Tell YOU Something Good...

_____

_____

_____

_____

_____

_____

_____

_____

I LOVE ME
Tell YOU Something Good...

_____

_____

_____

_____

_____

_____

_____

_____

I LOVE ME
Tell YOU Something Good…

_____

_____

_____

_____

_____

_____

_____

_____

Let's Write...
Date:

Let's Write...
Date:

_____
_____
_____
_____
_____
_____
_____
_____

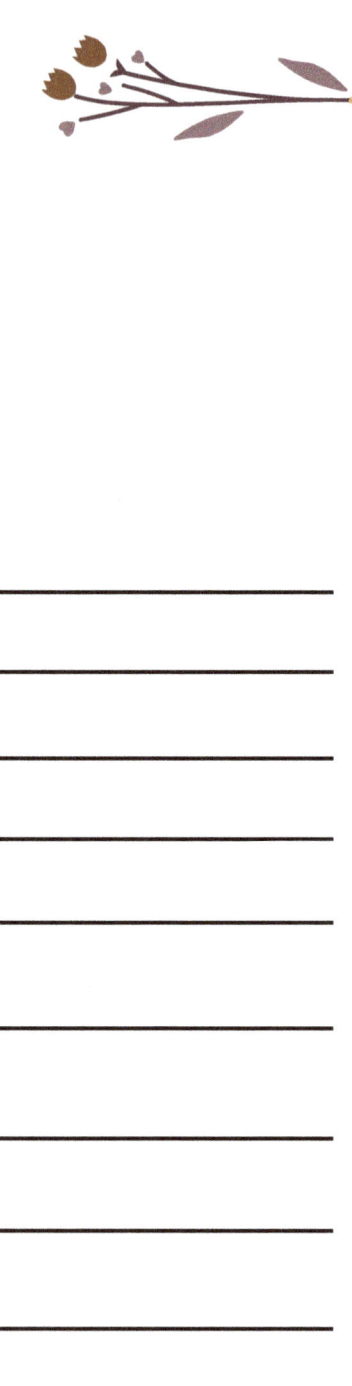

Let's Write...
Date:

_____

_____

_____

_____

_____

_____

_____

_____

Let's Write...
Date:

Let's Write...
Date:

Let's Write...
Date:

_____
_____
_____
_____
_____
_____
_____
_____
_____

Let's Write...
Date:

Let's Write...
Date:

Let's Write...
Date:

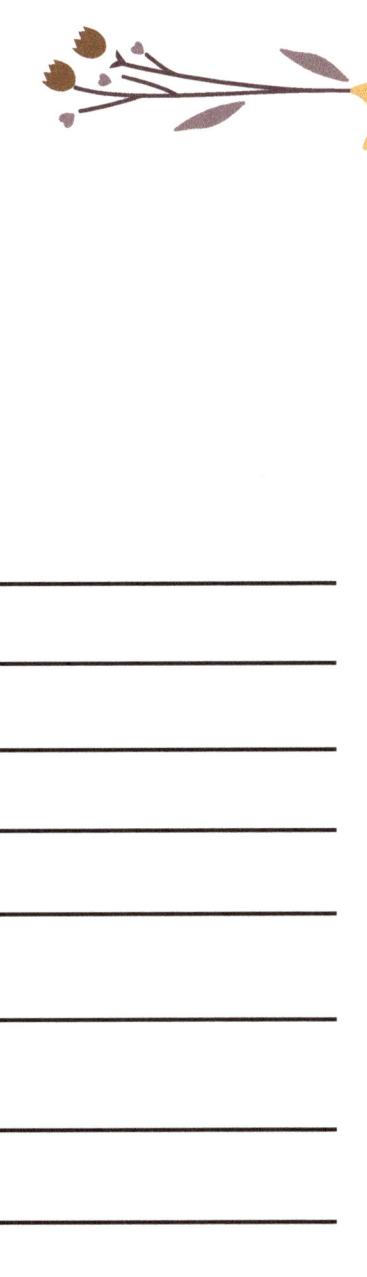

Let's Write...
Date:

Let's Write...
Date:

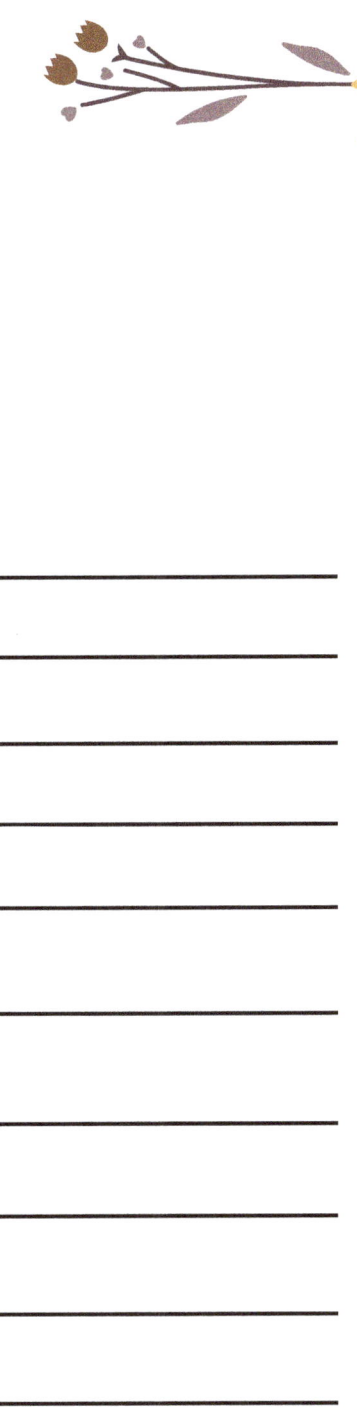

www.ingramcontent.com/pod-product-compliance
Lightning Source LLC
Chambersburg PA
CBHW062022290426
44108CB00024B/2746